Reflective Services

Reflective Services

40 quiet and gentle acts of worship

SUSAN SAYERS

kevin mayhew

kevin mayhew

First published in Great Britain in 1991, 1996 by Kevin Mayhew Ltd.
This edition published 2010.
Buxhall, Stowmarket, Suffolk IP14 3BW
Tel: +44 (0) 1449 737978 Fax: +44 (0) 1449 737834
E-mail: info@kevinmayhewltd.com

www.kevinmayhew.com

9 8 7 6 5 4 3 2 1 0

ISBN 978 1 84867 328 1
Catalogue No. 1501252

Cover design by Rob Mortonson
© Image used under licence from Shutterstock Inc.
Edited by Rebecca Henning
Typeset by Richard Weaver

Printed and bound in Great Britain

Contents

About the author

Susan is the author of many popular resource books for churches including our ever-popular *Living Stones* and *Confirmation Experience* series.

Through the conferences and workshops she is invited to lead, she has been privileged to share in the worship of many different traditions and cultures.

A teacher by profession, she has also been ordained a priest in the Anglican Church.

Other Susan Sayers Books

Living Stones series
Living Well series
Confirmation Experience series
1500 Prayers for Public Worship
Over 200 Talks for All-age Worship
Prayers of Intercession for Common Worship
300 Intercessions on Biblical Themes

Introduction

Reflective Services aims to provide a resource for parishes and ecumenical groups who want to have shared worship involving stillness, silence, music and reflection. The book contains 40 forms of worship, which nurture a deeper sense of wonder and adoration through enjoying the company of the Lord, and reflecting on many different facets of the nature of God.

Most of the services focus on particular qualities in the God we worship, such as wisdom, compassion or refreshment, and there are also themed services for morning and evening, and for particular occasions, such as conferences and parish meetings, reconciliation and rededication. Naturally the forms of worship vary considerably according to the theme, but all provide times of extended silence, Scripture reading, hymns and spoken exchanges between leaders and everyone else.

Many people are unused to silence, and need encouragement and help in settling to stillness and using it profitably, so direction is included for each time of silence. The length of silences can obviously be varied to suit the group and the occasion, but I feel that anything less than two minutes is really only a pause, and would not allow people sufficient time to get down into the silence and gain from it.

There should, if possible, be no exact beginning to the worship. Most of the services begin with a hymn – so to feel part of the constant wave of praise that continues all over the world as our planet turns, begin the singing with a small group before people start arriving. Then, as they come, there is no sense of waiting for a performance to start, but rather a sense of being drawn into the climate of worship which spans time and eternity.

If you are a small group in a large building, arrange a small area within it for everyone to be gathered, so as to emphasise that this is corporate worship – the body of Christ's people together. Think also about the most suitable way to arrange seating; a semicircle or square with space in the centre may be more helpful than long straight rows. Or, during good weather, you may like to try gathering somewhere outside.

The singing is an important part of the worship. Although it is lovely to have instrumental accompaniment, this is certainly not essential, so don't be deterred from singing because you have no accompanist available. Have one or two people to lead everyone in, and you may well find that the singing takes on new life.

It is often helpful to have flowers, foliage, candles, a picture, or some other focal point for people to use. This should always be arranged simply and prayerfully, and well in advance, so that there are no last-minute preparations going on when people start arriving. We need to create an atmosphere that is conducive to wholehearted worship and receptivity to God. To him be the glory.

Susan
Sayers
Reflective
Services
40 quiet and
gentle acts
of worship

Beginnings

As people are gathering, sing 'Wait for the Lord'.

Listen to the sounds around you. Be aware of your own breathing. Become aware of God's involvement with life and his living presence here at each 'now'.

Silence

Welcome, holy God, for we have gathered to meet you.
We have come to seek you.
To listen to you.
To worship you.
With the dust of life's journey on our feet, and the checklist of daily tasks still teeming in our mind, we come to settle ourselves at your feet and honour you above all else.

Listen to the words of Jesus, Son of the living God. He reminds us that there is a time for activity and work, and a time to be still and listen.

Reading Luke 10:38–42

This is the word of the Lord.
Thanks be to God.

Imagine yourself sitting at the feet of Jesus. You have chosen to put everything down and give him your whole attention. Remember that he has seen everything you ever did and he understands why you behave the way you do. In your imagination, look at his face and feel him communicating his love to you.

Silence

Father, as you look deep into our hearts
we acknowledge our need of your healing and forgiveness.

Silence

Father,
thank you for your total acceptance of where I am and who I am.

We call to mind the areas of tension and sadness in our life and in the lives of those we love.

Silence

Father,
let your will be accomplished here.

We call to mind our negative attitudes towards ourselves and others; our dreams and our disappointments.

Silence

Father,
you take us as we are. Make us fully ourselves as you long for us to be.

We call to mind the many reasons we have to be thankful.

Silence

Father,
my God and my all.
My God and my all.
My God and my all.

The Lord is my shepherd,
therefore shall I lack nothing.

The Lord is my stronghold;
of whom then shall I be afraid?

The Lord is my strength and my shield;
in him my heart trusts.

Hymn The Lord's my shepherd

May the stillness within us,
which comes from God and is God's indwelling,
stay with us, calm us and refresh us throughout each moment of our living.
Amen.

Finish with a shared Peace.

Morning

As people are gathering, sing 'Praise to the Lord, the Almighty'.

As the planet turns new voices wake to sing God's praise, and earth is circled with an unending chain of prayer.
Blessed be the unchanging God,
who already was in the beginning,
who is at this moment,
and who will be for ever.
Amen.

It was God who drew this day into light from darkness.
Blessed be God.
It is through God that we find ourselves living to see it.
Blessed be God.
It is with God that the richness of possibility unfolds.
Blessed be God.
For it is in God that we and all creation are held and cherished.
Blessed be God.

Become aware of the stillness of things around you. Match your own stillness to theirs – not a rigid, tight lack of movement, but a tranquil quietness of body. Be aware of your breathing, and the wavering of the candle flame which emphasises life in the stillness. Sense the pulse of God's love, holding all this together.

Silence

Be still and know that I am God.
O God, my God,
you are the source of all things,
you are the redeemer of all things,
you are the essence of all things.
In you I hope.
In you I become.
In you I live.

Reading Luke 12:22–31

This is the word of the Lord.
Thanks be to God.

With those words of Jesus making the journey from our ears to our heart, let us pray that in every household and family sharing this day
there may be tolerance and forgiveness,
patience and compassion,
and freedom from anxiety and fear.

Lord, in mercy,
hear us as we pray.

Silence

Father, we name before you in the silence of our hearts the households we represent, and those with whom our lives are linked.
Lord, in mercy,
hear us as we pray.

Silence

Father, we pray for those who are overwhelmed with pressure of work,
that there may be space for being,
and time for recreation.
Leader Lord, in mercy,
hear us as we pray.

Silence

We pray for those who are out of work,
that the flame of hope may not gutter
nor their perceived human value diminish.
Lord, in mercy,
hear us as we pray.

Silence

Hymn Be still and know that I am God

God of hope, fill us this day,
live in us, work in our lives,
and let your kingdom come.
Amen.

Finish with a shared Peace.

Evening

Shadows lengthen,
darkness thickens,
the lights are lit,
and the day we have lived through comes to an end.

Let us worship the God who separated light from darkness.
Hallowed be his name.
Let us worship the God who ordered the birth of stars.
Hallowed be his name.
Who watches over us, unsleeping, night and day.
Hallowed be his name.

Hymn Before the ending of the day

Feel the rhythm of your heartbeat and measured, regular breathing. Feel part of life's rhythm of being born, growing, ageing, dying and moving into eternal life. Feel this particular night as part of the rhythm of weeks, months and seasons. Feel in harmony with the creative, regenerating and sustaining life of God flowing through you.

Silence

Through our nights and days,
through our sleeping and waking,
through our resting and working,
keep us mindful of your presence, holy God.

Through places of darkness,
when we cannot see,
when we stumble,
keep us mindful of your faithful love.

When evil threatens,
deceiving and unnerving us,

masquerading as light,
keep us mindful of your strong protection.

We call to mind those whose shift is just beginning; those who are dreading this night;
Lord, have mercy.

We call to mind those who will have no shelter or adequate accommodation; those for whom the comfort of sleep does not come and whose minds cannot rest;
Lord, have mercy.

We call to mind those who will be severely tempted tonight to abuse or pollute their bodies; those for whom the night will drag past in pain; and those who, throughout the world, will die tonight.
Lord, have mercy.

Hymn Heaven shall not wait

Reading Psalm 121

This is the word of the Lord.
Thanks be to God.

We will lie down in peace and take our rest,
for it is you, Lord, who makes us dwell in safety.

Finish with a shared Peace.

Peace

As people are gathering to worship, sing 'Nada te turbe', continuing until everyone is still and relaxed. Then let the singing get quieter and quieter, so as to take you all down into God's stillness.

During the silence, breathe out the day's worries and pressure; breathe in the peace of eternal God.

Silence

'Peace I give you, my peace I give to you,' says the Lord.
Lord, give us your peace; *(pause)*
help us to accept the peace you give.
May your peace soak up our thoughts,
flood our feelings,
still our bodies,
fill this place.
In your peace let us relax, now,
accepting ourselves and each other
as you are accepting us.
Lord, give us your peace.

Think over the words you have just said, and allow God's peace to soak into you.

Silence

Hymn Peace, perfect peace

Listen to these words of Jesus and let them take root in you.

Reading Mark 4:35–41

This is the word of the Lord.
Thanks be to God.

Think over the words you have heard. Allow God to speak to your need for peace in the storms and worries of your own life. Allow him to take control over them and bring his calm into all areas of your life.

Silence

Enfolded in the beauty of peace let us pray to the Lord. For those who are full of anger, resentment and bitterness;

Silence

Lord, fill them with your peace.

For those who feel pressured, overworked and underappreciated;

Silence

Lord, fill them with your peace.

For those who feel burdened with guilt and who long for forgiveness;

Silence

Lord, fill them with your peace.

For those caught up in wars and political unrest, and who live in constant fear;

Silence

Lord, fill them with your peace.

For the desperately lonely who feel unwanted and unloved;

Silence

Lord, fill them with your peace.

God of Peace,
Flow through us and use us
as channels of your peace,
for the peace of the world.
Amen.

Hymn Peace is flowing like a river

May the peace of God be with you,
and may he also be with you.

Finish with a shared Peace.

Freedom

As you gather, sing 'Bless the Lord, my soul' until everyone is settled and joining in. Allow the singing to get quieter and quieter until God's silence can fill the gathering.

If the Son sets you free, then you will be really free.
If the Son sets us free, then we shall be really free.

Let your mind move over some of the many areas in our world where people are not really free. Think over some of the evils that trap, enslave and imprison them. Stand alongside them in their pain, in the presence of God.

Silence

Hymn Nada te turbe

A reading from the Gospel of John.

Reading John 8:31–36

This is the word of the Lord.
Thanks be to God.

Lord, we thirst for the freedom you offer;
we thirst for your perfect freedom,
which shatters our prisons of self and sin,
and scatters the shadows
of failure and fear.
Lord, God of true freedom,
come; set us free.

During the silence allow God to show you anything which is preventing you from living in his perfect freedom. Invite your Lord to break down all that still imprisons you and fetters your loving.

Silence

Hymn God forgave my sin

Lord, when you set us free
you set us free to serve;
free to expend our lives
in loving the hurt to wholeness,
in supporting the weak,
in striving for justice,
in breaking down prejudice.
in washing one another's feet.

When you set us perfectly free
you set us free to serve.

Offer yourself for God to use as a means of bringing his freedom to others.

Silence

Wrapped, with all creation, in the unlimited love of God, let us share the aching hearts of all who are denied basic human rights and have no power and no voice.

Silence

Lord, set them free.

Let us share the pain of those who are abused and tortured and imprisoned for their conscience's sake.

Silence

Lord, set them free.

Let us share the grief of those who must watch their children die from starvation and disease.

Silence

Lord, set them free.

Let us share the joy of all who are freed from pain, poverty and injustice;
and let us rejoice in all
whose generous lives
are poured out freely in love
for the good of the world.
Amen.

Hymn Make me a channel of your peace

Finish with a shared Peace.

Stillness

As you are gathering sing 'Be still, for the presence of the Lord' until everyone is still and attentive to God.

Soak yourself in this silence. Don't spend it waiting for whatever comes next, but immerse yourself in the present moment. Absorb the stillness and silence until it is both around you and within you.

Silence

In a world vibrating with action
we have come here to be still.
In a world of tight schedules and deadlines
we have come to absorb the present.
In a world of limits and frustrations
we have come to the brink of eternity.
At the still point of our churning world
we can meet the unchanging God
and know his peace.

You may find it helpful to think those words over again slowly.

Silence

Hymn Stay with me

You are here in the heart of God's stillness. Don't force yourself to say anything or pray anything. Allow God to make his stillness deeply known in your body, your mind and your spirit.

Silence

Hymn Holy, holy, holy is the Lord

Oh Lord, our God,
you have created all things,
and you hold all things in existence.
Each moment is touched with your love,
each moment expresses your truth.

Through time and eternity,
YOU ARE. And we worship you.

Hymn I love you, Lord

Listen, now, and hear the words of Jesus, spoken to the Pharisees.

Reading John 8:56–58

This is the word of the Lord.
Thanks be to God.

Recognise that all your past can be brought into the everlasting presence of God; offer him any memories which are painful, so that he can heal them and transform them.

Silence

Hymn O Lord, your tenderness

We pray now for all who need God's stillness in their lives; for those who are anxious about many things; those for whom even little worries loom very large.

Silence

Lord, give them peace in your stillness.

For those who have too much to do and too little time to do it thoroughly;

Silence

Lord, give them peace in your stillness.

For those who are unnerved by solitude and those who are desperately lonely;

Silence

Lord, give them peace in your stillness;
give all of us your lasting peace.
Amen.

Finish with a shared Peace.

Compassion

As people are gathering, sing 'Bless the Lord, my soul'. You are entering into ongoing worship, rather than hanging around waiting for a performance to start. As people arrive, they should settle into stillness and join in the singing when they are ready to.

Think over the things in your life which you know need healing or changing. God has the power and the desire to rescue you.

Silence

Lord, when we are still far off,
you see us and run to welcome us.
When we panic and start sinking,
your arms are quick to hold us up.
When we get lost and wander aimlessly,
you never stop searching
until you have found us.
And so we come to worship you,
for you are our Good Shepherd,
and we are the sheep of your pasture.

Hymn Do not be afraid

Listen. Our God is among us as he has promised. With love he reaches out to us, person to person.
Lord, we receive your love.

Do not fill the silence with output to God. Be still in body and spirit and leave the output to God – allow your Lord to accept you and love you as his precious child.

Silence

Listen now to these words from Matthew and Luke's Gospels. Listen not only with your ears, but with your heart as well.

Readings Matthew 9:35, 36; Luke 5:12, 13

Say after each reading:
This is the word of the Lord.
Thanks be to God.

Remember times when you have felt compassion for someone – a rush of love and a longing to help them. Remember times when you have been loved and rescued by someone.

Silence

It is the very nature of our God to feel for those in distress and long to help them. So we bring to him now all those finding life bewildering, chaotic and out of their control.

Silence

May they find shelter under your wings.

We bring to him those who are disillusioned, and have given up hope.

Silence

May they feel you reaching out to their need.

We bring to you those who have been persuaded that they are not worth bothering with.

Silence

May they blossom, convinced that they are loved.

We bring to you those who have been taught by abuse never to trust.

Silence

May they be healed by your faithfulness.

Lord, it is through our hands that they will know your love;
God of compassion,
forgive us for failing to pass on
the love you give us so freely.
Enable us and use us
to bring your love to the world.
Amen.

Hymn Spirit of the living God

As we have known the compassion of God,
we will strive to live with compassion
for all his sheep and lambs.

Finish with a shared Peace.

Wisdom

As you gather, sing 'God be in my head'. This can be sung over several times, until everyone is settled and attentive to God.

During the time of silence acknowledge each thought that floats up to the surface of your mind and 'hand it over' to God. Allow his peace to fill your mind.

Silence

Lord, to whom else could we go?
You alone have the words of eternal life.
We ask you to open our minds to greater possibilities;
to push back the margins of our understanding.
To think your thoughts
and look with your eyes.

Oh Lord our God, to whom else could we go?
You alone have the words of eternal life.

Hymn Do not be afraid

Enjoy being in the companionship of the God who knows you and loves you.

Silence

Listen and hear these words from the book of Job.

Reading Job 28:12–28

This is the word of the Lord.
Thanks be to God.

There is so much in our world to confuse and distress us;
so much that we do not understand.

You say that to be wise we need to have reverence for the Lord of Wisdom.
To understand we need to turn from evil.

We ask you, Lord, to help us see the evil that is in our lives, and in our world.

We ask you to give us courage to face it,
reject it and fight against it.

Be relaxed yet alert in the silence, allowing your will to be realigned to God's will, so that you are open to receive any guidance, pricks of conscience or reassurance from the God of Wisdom.

Silence

Let us pray together now for a deeper awareness of God's wisdom in our world. For all whose lives are confused and bewildering; for those who can see no sense in life;

Silence

Lord, may your wisdom teach us understanding.

For those who see God's wisdom as foolishness; for those who entrust their security to what is perishable;

Silence

Lord, may your wisdom show us where lasting treasure is found.

For all in positions of authority and responsibility, throughout the world;

Silence

Lord, may your wisdom give insight and integrity.

For those who find it hard to make decisions; for those paying dearly for past mistakes;

Silence

Lord, may your wisdom work in us for good, in every situation.

Lord, God of Wisdom,
realign our minds and hearts and wills
to be at one with you,
in all we think, and feel and do.
Amen.

Hymn All heaven declares

Finish with a shared Peace.

Healing

As you gather, sing 'Be still and know that I am God', so that as people arrive they can join in. Each time it is repeated recognise, a little more clearly, the wonder and healing power of God.

Take time to be aware of how your body is working automatically to keep you alive:
breathe naturally but notice the breathing;
be aware of your heartbeat, too.
Let us be thankful for being alive.

Silence

Lord God, source of life,
we rejoice that through the power
of your love we are alive;
breathing, thinking, feeling creatures,
made in your likeness
and for your glory.

Lord God, source of life,
recognising that our life exists
through your desire.
we thank you and praise you
and glorify you.

Hymn Laudate Dominum

Listen now, both with ears and hearts, to these words from Luke's Gospel.

Reading Luke 5:12, 13

This is the word of the Lord.
Thanks be to God.

Think over the reading. Imagine the scene with the crowds, and all the colours, sights, sounds and smells. Imagine how the leper was feeling as he approached Jesus. Imagine how he felt when he said to Jesus, 'If you want to you can make me clean.' Think how encouraging and loving Jesus is. Hear Jesus saying these words to you: 'I do want to! Be clean.'

Silence

Lord, it is always your will to bring us to wholeness.
We ask that your healing love
will enfold, soothe, support and comfort
all who are ill or in pain.

Especially we pray for . . . *(Particular people can be named before God. Time for prayer should be given between each name – they should not be read as a list. Any of those present can feel free to add other names.)*

Hymn O Lord, hear my prayer

Pray in this silence for those who minister God's love, and for those God is longing to make whole and free.

Silence

During the next hymn there can be prayer ministry, anointing or laying on of hands.

Hymn Peace is flowing like a river

As the healing ministry draws to a close:

All praise and thanks be to our God who loves us to wholeness!
All praise and thanks be to our God,
to the Lord who saves us, Alleluia!

Finish with a shared Peace.

Listening

As you gather sing 'O Lord, hear my prayer'.

Be aware of the stillness of your surroundings and yourself as choosing to share stillness. Know that you are held in being, in the present, by the presence and will of God. Listen to the still moment God has called you to share with him.

Silence

In the confusion and noise of living
you listen and hear our secret thoughts.
Amid the endless battering of words
you listen and hear our unspoken longings.

Through the barrage of anger and misunderstanding
you listen and hear the pain that we hide.
You hear the grieving of those who are mourning:
you hear the joy of lovers and friends.
You hear the cheep of each sparrow in danger:
you hear the bleat of each lamb who is lost.

In our threats
you hear our fear;
in our jealousy
you hear our cry to be valued;
in our lack of forgiveness
you hear our need to be forgiven.
And so we can come before you in honesty and simplicity, without pretence or exaggeration,
for you have heard us already and know
our needs, our longings and our fears,
and we can trust you with what is most
precious to us – ourselves.

Think over what you have been saying, and trust God with your whole self. 'You are my child, and I love you,' says the Lord.

Silence

Some words to comfort us from the Psalms.

Readings Psalm 116:1–7; Psalm 91:14–16

Say after each reading:
This is the word of the Lord.
Thanks be to God.

Listen to God welcoming you. In the quietness, bring to him all that lies heavily on your heart.

Silence

Let us pray together now for those who have no one to talk to; no one to turn to for support.

Silence

Lord, hear us, and supply our needs.

We pray for all those who are misunderstood and unfairly treated.

Silence

Lord, hear us, and supply our needs.

We pray for those who are deaf, and all who have difficulty speaking and making their needs known.

Silence

Lord hear us, and supply our needs.

We pray for those who feel powerless and ineffectual; those who are denounced for speaking out for what is right because it is unpopular.

Silence

Lord, hear us, and supply our needs.

We pray for all who are learning to speak, and all who are learning to pray.

Silence

Thank you, Lord, for listening to us,
now and at all times.
Help us to listen as you do:
compassionately, open-mindedly, patiently,
and with our whole attention.
Amen.

Hymn Make me a channel of your peace

Finish with a shared Peace.

Surrender

As you are gathering, sing 'From heaven you came'.

Allow God to teach you about himself through the words and music you have been singing and through the people around you whom he has chosen and called.

Silence

Most holy God, the heavens and the earth are full of your glory;
all glory be to you, oh Lord most high!

Hymn All heaven declares

Put aside all thoughts linked with yourself and your life, and focus your love and thankfulness on the God of glory. Worship him with your mind, your heart and your strength.

Silence

All-powerful Lord,
we honour you.
Lord of the universe and all creation,
we offer you our praise.
Lord of all time and distance,
we worship and adore you.

Hymn Adoramus te, Domine

It is not only those of you here now who are praising and adoring. You are part of a vast number, both on earth and in heaven, who are worshipping God because he is truly worthy of our worship.

Silence

Listen now to a reading from Paul's letter to the Philippians.

Reading Philippians 2:5–11

This is the word of the Lord.
Thanks be to God.

Lord, we thank you
that you were willing to surrender everything,
even your life,
in order to save us
and set us free from sin.
We thank you
that you are Master, and yet you
come among us as one who serves.

Think over all that the God of glory surrendered in order to become human and bring us abundant life. Think of the risks he took in doing so.

Silence

Hymn My song is love unknown

Keeping in mind Christ's willingness to surrender himself in complete obedience to the way of Love, we pray
that we may be given courage
to relinquish our grip on what we possess,
so that we could gladly surrender
anything that might be required of us.

Silence

We pray
that in our time, our talents and our resources
we may be more ready to give,
and more willing to share.

Silence

We pray
that we may really place each day
at God's disposal, so that he can truly use us
in the way he needs to,
rather than in the way we choose.

Silence

We pray
that whenever we are forced to surrender
our money, time or energy unexpectedly,
we may not grumble at the inconvenience,
but rejoice at the privilege.

Silence

We pray
that you will enable us to give ourselves
completely away in order to enjoy
the richness of possessing Christ.
Amen.

Allow God to show you any parts of your life which have become too important to you; or any situations or people who need more of your time or resources than you are giving. Don't force this, making 'helpful' suggestions to God about it – you need only to be receptive to whatever he brings to mind.

Silence

Hymn For the healing of the nations

Let us go now
in the power of the Lord;
delighting in the privilege
of being no more than servants.

Finish with a shared Peace.

Susan Sayers
Reflective Services
40 quiet and gentle acts of worship

Harmony

If possible, as you gather, let each person take a candle and light it, placing it round a globe or on a map of the world. While this is going on, everyone is singing 'Jesus, remember me'.

In the quietness, think over the words 'Love your neighbour as yourself', repeating them from time to time.

Silence

Humankind looks on the outward appearance
but God looks on the heart.

God knows us better than we know ourselves;
God understands us better
than we understand ourselves.
As a parent he watches us
take our first steps;
he is there, ready to pick us up
when we fall down.

As our brother he has known
the cruellest temptation;
as our Saviour he has power
to break our chains of sin.

During the silence, call to mind one or two areas in your life where you have failed to keep the two great commandments – to love God, and to love your neighbour as yourself.

Silence

Sin is a barrier which cuts us off from God. Let us trust our Loving Father even with the parts of us we are ashamed to admit.
Loving Father, we are sorry
for all our barriers of sin
which block us off from you
and from each other.
We ask you to dissolve these barriers away.
and keep them down. Amen.

Hymn Amazing grace

Listen to these words from the first letter of John.

Reading 1 John 1:3–9

This is the word of the Lord.
Thanks be to God.

During this time of silence, reflect on the words of the reading, accepting that God has completely forgiven us – we are truly free, and are already being healed of the damage sin has caused.

Silence

Our world is greatly damaged by sin. Let us pray together for those living together in strained and difficult relationships; for those brought up in an atmosphere of mutual antagonism and distrust.

Silence

Come among them, Lord, with your peace.

For longstanding family feuds and unforgiven hurts; for all who are rejected and insulted.

Silence

Come among them, Lord, with your love.

For the gap of understanding between those of different cultures, colours and faiths: for our divided world.

Silence

Come among us, Lord, with your openness.

Lord, we thank you
that you have the power to reconcile
us to you and to each other.

Lord, we ask you
to keep us in this love,
ready to be servants
and peacemakers
whatever the personal cost.
Amen.

Finish with a shared Peace.

Reconciliation

No one is beyond the reach of God's love and mercy.
Nothing is beyond God's forgiveness.
Nothing we do can make God love us less.
Nothing we do can make God love us more.

O God, three in one,
both creative and redeeming,
both giver and given,
we worship you.

Hymn Be thou my guardian and my guide

Let us call to mind the sin that grieves the heart of God.

As you still your body and quieten your mind, become aware of God's attentiveness to you. He loves you, knows the difficulties of your life, and understands why you behave the way you do. He is not poised to condemn. He is not about to frighten you or reject you. Bring to mind all that is burdening your heart.

Silence

Hymn Forgive our sins as we forgive

Lord God, Maker and Saviour,
I have examined my conscience
in the light of your presence.
I have brought to mind all that causes you pain,
all that burdens my life with guilt and regret.
I confess to you that I have sinned against your love, in what I have done
and in what I have failed to do.
I am sorry for the grief I have caused you,
and the pain I have caused your children.
More than anything, I long to be forgiven,
for my sin to be hurled into the depths of the sea.

I long for a fresh start,
and the opportunity to show you my love
in the way that I live my life.
Amen.

God has promised that when two or three are gathered together in his name, he will grant their requests. We believe in his promise and know that he forgives all who turn to him in penitence.
He forgives us, and takes away our sin.
All praise and thanks to God,
who alone can forgive us our sins.
All praise and thanks to God,
whose love has set us free.

Lord, into our failings
you breathe forgiveness.
Into our heartaches
you breathe your solace.
Into our confusion
you breathe reassurance.
Into our disappointments
you breathe encouragement.
Into our anxiety
you breathe courage.
Into our clutter
you breathe your priorities.
Into our loneliness
you breathe your companionship.
Into our living
you breathe your life.

Reading Ephesians 6:10–17

This is the word of the Lord.
Thanks be to God.

Let us go in the peace and strength of Christ.
Amen.

Glory

As you gather, sing 'Hosanna, hosanna'. Pray the words as you sing them, so that the singing is a true act of praise and thanksgiving.

Glory to God!
Glory to God. Glory to God in the highest!

Hymn Adoramus te, Domine

Delight in giving all honour and praise to the only One in all time and space who deserves it. You may find it helpful, in starting off, to repeat these words slowly and thoughtfully:
Glory be to the Father
and to the Son
and to the Holy Spirit.
As it was in the beginning,
is now and shall be for ever.
Amen.

Silence

Lord, how can we ever thank you enough for all that you are and all that you have done?
We praise you for the wonder
of all that lives and grows;
we praise you for pattern and order,
the complex and the simple.
The whole universe reflects your glory.

From the wideness of space, to the detail of cells;
from the rainbow to the raindrop,
from the frog to the whale;
the whole universe reflects your glory,
and we worship you.

Picture some of the landscapes of the world you find especially beautiful or which have particularly special memories for you, and give God the praise and glory for them.

Silence

A reading from Psalm 145.

Reading Psalm 145:1–13

This is the word of the Lord.
Thanks be to God.

Hymn This world you have made

Repeat these words from time to time as you think over the glory of God shown in the perfect loving, caring, healing life of Jesus: 'And we beheld his glory, the glory as of the only begotten Son of the Father, full of grace and truth.'

Silence

Let us pray together for the world God loves so much. For those who lavish affection on things that can never fully satisfy;

Silence

Lord, may your glory fill the earth.

For those who have become disillusioned with worldly values, and have not yet discovered where true value lies;

Silence

Lord, may your glory fill the earth.

For a misguided world which reckons human worth in terms of earning potential, and parades greed as enterprise;

Silence

Lord, may your glory fill the earth.

Glorious in majesty, holy and almighty,
we worship you, our Lord and God,
through time and through all eternity.
Amen.

Hymn My God, how wonderful thou art

Finish with a shared Peace.

Love

As everyone is gathering, sing 'Ubi caritas' until there is stillness, and attention is focused on the God of Love.

As distractions drift up to the top of your mind, acknowledge them and put them to one side. As worries and anxious thoughts occur, hand them over to God. As feelings of guilt or regret emerge, tell God about it and let him know you are sorry. Allow him to forgive you.

Silence

Wherever love is, there is God.
What kind of love is God's love?
It is love that forgives
and then forgives
and forgives again.

It is love that rolls up its sleeves
and gets involved with caring
and mending and building.
It is love that is quite happy
to be considered a fool,
to be considered weak.
It is love that goes on giving
but keeps no accounts;
love that is non-selective
and unconditional.

This is the nature of God's love
for this is the nature of our God.

Hymn Father, we adore you

Thank God for the way he loves you unconditionally, even when he knows the worst as well as the best about you! Now bask in the warmth and affection of his love.

Silence

Let us listen now to these words about the nature of love, from Paul's letter to the Christians in Corinth.

Reading 1 Corinthians 13:1–7

This is the word of the Lord.
Thanks be to God.

Hymn A new commandment

God is Love. Think over the reading about love, so as to understand more about the character of God.

Silence

Lord; how amazing your love for us must be, since you were willing to become one with us and even to die for us.
Lord, how amazing your love for us must be!

Hymn Such love

Knowing God's immense love for us all, let us bring to mind all who are feeling unloved and unwanted;

Silence

Lord, let them know your love for them.

All who are being taught to hate;

Silence

Lord, let them know
your unconditional love.

All who thirst for your faithful, accepting love, and do not realise it is freely available to them;

Silence

Lord, lead them to experience your love.

All who, seeing only our poor example, reject the God we claim to serve;

Silence

Lord, may the light of our love so shine to others
that they are drawn to know
the joy of your love for themselves.
Amen.

Hymn Lord, the light of your love is shining

Finish with a shared Peace.

Courage

As you gather, sing 'When I needed a neighbour'.

The Lord's love is surely not exhausted, nor has his compassion failed;
they are new every morning,
so great is his constancy.
'The Lord', I say, 'is all that I have;
therefore I shall wait for him patiently.'
Lamentations 3:22–24

Think of yourself walking slowly and expectantly into the deep place within you where God dwells. Put down outside the usual details and practicalities of today. They will be looked after for you, and will still be there when you return. For now you are setting out to wait on God; to be attentive to his loving will; and he is waiting for you.

Silence

We come to you, the One, True, Living God,
with our hands empty and open,
our hearts attentive,
and our spirits willing.

We come to you
thirsting for all that is right
and loving and good;
hungering to understand you more;
ready to do your will.

Listen, then, to the words of Jesus.

Reading John 13:34, 35

This is the word of the Lord.
Thanks be to God.

Hymn Help us to help each other, Lord

The loving that Jesus commands is costly. Let us pray fervently for God's love to enable and equip us for the loving he asks of us.

Father, we ask you to prise open our closed hearts and risk the kind of loving you showed us through Jesus.

Silence

Lord, we believe in your power;
help us where our faith falls short.

Father, we ask you for the courage to make loving decisions which may hurt.

Silence

Lord, we believe in your power;
help us where our faith falls short.

Father, we ask you to open our eyes to see what people's real needs are and how we can help them.

Silence

Lord, we believe in your power;
help us where our faith falls short.

Father, we ask you to transform our minds so that we think lovingly in every situation and in every potential argument.

Silence

Lord, we believe in your power;
help us where our faith falls short.

Father, we thank you
for the steadfast, faithful love you have for each of us.
We thank you
for your perseverence and patience with each of us.
We thank you
for the prospect of living in harmony with you from this moment,
through all the moments till death,
and in your eternity.

May God who has met us here and welcomed us be always welcome in our hearts and homes.
Amen.

Finish with a shared Peace.

Joy

As you are gathering, sing 'Jubilate, everybody'. This can be sung as a round once enough people have arrived.

Thank you, Lord, our God,
for the pleasure of your company:
for the companionship of your friends
for the happiness of singing
your praise together.

Lord, we ask you
to free us in our praise
so that we may enjoy to the full
receiving what you delight to give us,
and giving what you delight to receive.

Hymn I will enter his gates

Enjoy being in the company of your Saviour, who is happy to share this time with you. Talk with him if you wish, but you don't have to say anything at all; it may help to think of yourself as young child just leaning against a loving parent.

Silence

It was with joy that Mary sang;
it was news of great joy
which the angels proclaimed.

With joy the shepherd finds his lost sheep,
the woman her lost coin,
the ploughman his hidden treasure.
The kingdom of God
is a kingdom of joy –
a deep delight which lasts for ever
and is for ever renewed:
a freshwater spring
that never runs dry.
Lord, give us this joy.

The more we are turned in on ourselves, the less we will notice God's joy. Use this silence to turn deliberately away from self-centredness towards God-centredness. You will find any resentment, bitterness or annoyance beginning to lift; the space it leaves will be filled with God's joy.

Silence

Lord, the joy that you provide
is independent of mood, food or treats.
Your joy runs deeper than rapids;
it is beyond the range of all pain;
your joy is promised
and brings great happiness;
yet it is quite compatible with tears.

Listen now to these words from Isaiah.

Reading Isaiah 35:1–10

This is the word of the Lord.
Thanks be to God.

So let us pray together in the joy and comfort of knowing God's love for us, for all who weep and mourn at the moment.

Silence

May their sorrow be turned into joy.

For all who suffer from depression and mental anguish;

Silence

May their suffering be redeemed and used for good.

For those whose happiness is dependent on status and money;

Silence

May they know your lasting joy.

For all who work to alleviate suffering;

Silence

The fruit of the Spirit
is love, joy, and peace.
May God, the source of hope,
fill us with all joy and peace.
Amen.

Finish with a shared Peace.

Friendship

As you are gathering, sing 'Stay with me'. As people arrive, they can join in with the ongoing worship when they are ready to.

With thankfulness, let us think over some of our own friends and the qualities of their friendship which we really appreciate.

Silence

Lord, we thank you
for the companions you have given us
and the friendships we enjoy.
We thank you for those
we can laugh and cry with,
for those we relax with,
for those we are most comfortable with
because they accept us
and like us
as we are.

Lord, we are sorry
for the times we have let our friends down;
expected too much of them,
or too little.

We are sorry
that sometimes our selfishness
causes friction and sadness.

Lord, we ask you
to bless our friendships
and fill them
with your love.

Hymn Will you come and follow me

Jesus calls us to be his friends – his companions. Are you willing to go with him? Allow God to remind you of some of the things which hold you back. Ask him to help you respond to his call.

Silence

Hymn I, the Lord of sea and sky

Listen. Hear these words of Jesus, from John's Gospel. Listen not only with your ears, but with your heart as well.

Reading John 15:10–17

This is the word of the Lord.
Thanks be to God.

Jesus said, 'You are my friend if you do what I command you . . . my command is that you love one another.' Enjoy being in the company of your Friend.

Silence

Jesus, our Saviour and our friend, we pray for all who are persecuted, sneered at, or ignored because they are your friends.

Silence

Lord, may they know
you are very close to them.

We pray for those who used to be your friends but who walk no longer in your company.

Silence

Lord, may they be reminded
of your love and faithfulness.

We pray for the children who are never introduced to you.

Silence

Lord, may they be led to know you.

We pray for all who need befriending.

Silence

Lord,
make us instruments of your peace,
so that many are drawn
to know the joy of your friendship.
Amen.

Finish with a shared Peace.

Journeying

As you gather, sing 'O for a closer walk with God'.

Think over the promise Jesus has made to us: 'Look, I am with you always; yes, to the end of time.' It may help to repeat this from time to time as we let God show us how it affects us and our lives.

Silence

We are a pilgrim people.
A travelling people; followers of the Way.

And 'I am the Way', says the Lord.
Lord, not only do you lead the way;
you are the Way.
Through you, and in you,
is the Way of love;
through you, and in you
is the Way of life.

Hymn The Lord is my light

Whatever the terrain of your life-journey, you can walk it in the company of Jesus, so that he becomes your route. Allow him to take over the navigation from this moment. From now on, you will be travelling on him, in him and with him.

Silence

Lord, you have always led your people, and travelled with them.
You called Abraham from the city to the desert.
Jacob discovered your closeness
in his loneliness as he fled from Esau;
as Moses and the people of Israel
travelled in the wilderness,
you went before them always –
a pillar of cloud by day,
and by night a pillar of fire.

No darkness is too dark for you;
no depth or height is beyond your reach.
You are there at our going out and our coming in
from this time forward for evermore.

Hymn Nada te turbe

Think of the occasions and situations in your life which you dread, or when you know you are often tempted to behave unlovingly. Ask for the Lord to protect and guide you through these dangerous areas of your journey.

Silence

We have God's promise that he will be with us always. Listen to these words of encouragement to us from the book of Isaiah.

Reading Isaiah 43:1–7

This is the word of the Lord.
Thanks be to God.

Thank God for his promise, and know that he will definitely keep it. Even through the valley of the shadow of death we need not be afraid. He will be with us, keeping us safe.

Silence

Let us pray together now for those who are coming near to the end of their earthly journey.

Silence

Father, may they know
the comfort of your presence.

For those who have lost their way and can't get out of the mess they have got themselves into;

Silence

Father, search for them, and carry them home.

For those whose lives are at a crossroads, with important decisions to make about direction;

Silence

Father, counsel them and show them the way.

We thank you, Lord,
for your faithfulness
and your constant love.
As we journey,
you are our strength
and our song!

Hymn O Jesus, I have promised

Finish with a shared Peace.

Susan
Sayers
Reflective
Services
40 quiet and
gentle acts
of worship

Hope

As you gather, sing 'Peace, perfect peace, is the gift' until settled and attentive to God.

Think over some of the things about our world which make you feel sad, or which disturb you. Think of areas where you feel powerless to change things for the better.

Silence

Lord, in our weakness,
we come to you for strength.
In our blindness,
we come to you for sight.
In our desire for good to be accomplished,
we come to you,
the source of all goodness.
In our longing for the coming of the Kingdom,
we approach you, the King of kings.

Lord, our God,
your light dispels all darkness,
your springs make deserts blossom;
the warmth of your love
melts what is frozen,
restores what was lost,
refreshes what was weary.

In you, Lord God, there is always hope,
because you have overcome sin and death,
and opened to us the gates of heaven.

Hymn Just as I am, without one plea

In the peace of this stillness, still your body and mind. Allow God to fill you with his peace; peace of mind and peace of spirit. Things may seem hopeless to us, but 'with God all things are possible'.

Silence

Listen now to these words from Paul's letter to the Ephesians.

Reading Ephesians 1:11–20

This is the word of the Lord.
Thanks be to God.

Hope is not a doubtful wish; it is a joyful certainty about the future. Ask that God will increasingly open your mind to see this hope which he has called you to.

Silence

Hymn Do not be afraid

Heavenly Father, knowing that you love us, we come to you with our needs and concerns. We bring to your love our desire for deeper faith, and a clearer understanding of your will for us.

Silence

Lord, you are our hope and our strength.

We bring to your love our reluctance to trust you and our longing to trust you more.

Silence

Lord, you are our hope and our strength.

We bring to your love all who rely and depend on us, and our concern not to let them down.

Silence

Lord, you are our hope and our strength.

We bring to your love the areas of our life which have become too precious to us, and our desire to serve you alone.

Silence

Lord, you are our hope and our strength,
and we put our trust in you.

Hymn Nada te turbe

Finish with a shared Peace.

Sorrow

As you gather, sing 'Jesus, remember me' until everyone is attentive to God, in stillness.

We are bound to have brought here with us some of the pressure and busyness of life. Allow God to quieten not just your body but your mind and spirit as well. Breathe in his peace; breathe out all hurry and tension.

Silence

Lord, we lay at your feet
all that we are,
all that we have been,
and all that we could become.

Because we can come to you honestly,
and because we can trust you
not to reject us,
we have come to confide in you
our secret pains and sorrows,
our nagging doubts, and regrets,
and our deepest fears.

Confide in the God who made you, understands you and loves you. Tell him about those things which weigh heavily on your heart.

Silence

Listen now to these words from the book of Isaiah.

Reading Isaiah 53:1–6

This is the word of the Lord.
Thanks be to God.

The God we worship is also the man of sorrows, and acquainted with grief.
He shares in the depth
of each personal sorrow;
he shares in the deepest darkness of pain;
he shares in the anguished face of the tortured,
the starving, the rejected, the oppressed.

So, Lord, in our sorrow
we cry to you for help:
for the exhausted and the lonely,
for the crippled and the weak;
for the frightened and the slandered,
for the desperate and the poor.
Lord, in mercy, come to our aid.

Hymn O Lord, hear my prayer

Hear, now, these words of comfort from Paul's letter to the Romans.

Reading Romans 8:35–39

This is the word of the Lord.
Thanks be to God.

Think over the amazing power and capacity of God's love for you. It is large enough to take the suffering of every person in every generation. Lean on that love, and allow it to sustain and refresh you.

Silence

Hymn Adoramus te, Domine

Immeasurably powerful must your love be, O Lord;
willingly taking our suffering upon you;
dying that we may be brought to new life.
Lord, may we thank you
and praise you for ever,
both in our words,
and the way that we live.

Lord, anoint us to love with your loving, sharing one another's burdens and bearing the light of your hope to the world. Amen.

Hymn You shall go out with joy

Finish with a shared Peace.

Unity

While you are gathering, sing 'Adoramus te, Domine' until everyone is settled and attentive to God.

It takes time to become 'collected', even within ourselves. By focusing your attention on these words, 'Jesus, we are here for you', allow your body, your mind and your spirit to be united in worshipping God.

Silence

Jesus, you have drawn us here
from different places
and from different backgrounds,
to unite us in your love.

Lord, we acknowledge
that in many ways our lives lack unity.
Between the ideals and the pressures
there is compromise;
between the dreams and the realities
there are frustrations;
between the belief and the expression
there is misunderstanding and conflict.

So, Lord. we turn to you to unite us:
to whom else could we go?
You alone have the words of eternal life!
As we centre our lives on you,
Melt our divisions and make us one.

Hymn O Lord, your tenderness

Don't try to fill the next silence with thoughts, however holy. Hold yourself still, relaxed but attentive, so that God can fill you and work his healing in you.

Silence

Let us listen now to part of Jesus' prayer for the apostles, just before he was crucified.

Reading John 17:11b–23

This is the word of the Lord.
Thanks be to God.

Hymn Bind us together, Lord

Brothers and sisters in Christ, let us pray together for the millions, all over the world, who have come to know Jesus as Lord.

Silence

May we all be one,
as you and the Father are one.

For the leaders and pastors of the different churches;

Silence

May we all be one,
as you and the Father are one.

We thank you for the joy of worshipping together, and the privilege of serving the same Master.

Silence

May we all be one,
as you and the Father are one.

We offer you every opportunity for praying and working together, so that you can use us to your glory.

Silence

May we all be one,
as you and the Father are one.

By your arms outstretched in love for us on the cross,
draw us to love and forgive one another;
draw us to be less thrown by our difference,
and more encouraged by what we hold in common.

Breathe through us, Holy Spirit,
renew us and revive us,
until all people come to worship you.
Amen.

Hymn Laudate Dominum

Finish with a shared Peace.

Persecution

As you are gathering, sing 'Stay with me'. When people arrive, they can join in with the ongoing worship as soon as they are ready.

You may think you are here just because you decided to come. But you are also here because God chose you to be. Be still and attentive to him now.

Silence

We have come to spend time watching and praying with Christ.
Lord, in the garden of Gethsemane
you asked your friends
to watch with you and pray.

In agony of spirit you prayed,
knowing the terrible ordeal that was before you;
knowing the hate in the eyes
of those who wanted you dead;
knowing the vulnerability of love.

Greater love has no man than this,
that he will lay down his life for his friends.

Imagine that agony of Gethsemane. Be relaxed in your body and alert in your spirit, so that you can watch and pray with the persecuted Christ.

Silence

Hymn My song is love unknown

Listen to this great teaching of Jesus about persecution and suffering.

Reading Matthew 5:3–12

This is the word of the Lord.
Thanks be to God.

Do you rejoice when you are ridiculed or insulted on account of following Jesus? Let the full impact of this teaching take root in you, until you can consider any such antagonism, however small, a great privilege.

Silence

Loving is always expensive.
When we love, we put ourselves at risk;
we are no longer insulated
against pain and rejection.
Loving is an expensive way to live.

Loving is also rewarding.
No other way fulfils us;
no other way gives us peace and joy.
Only love can set our lives free.

Hymn Do not be afraid

You will be given all the strength and resources you need for doing God's will. Allow him to equip you now for whatever he has in mind for you to do and be.

Silence

Let us pray together now for all children who are badly treated, neglected or abused.

Silence

Lord, as their suffering wounds you,
may it also wound us to work
for their protection and comfort.

For those with special needs, who are vulnerable; and easy prey to the unscrupulous;

Silence

Lord, as you understand their needs,
and care for them, may we, too,
understand their needs and care for them.

For all whom society prefers to ignore;

Silence

Lord, as you consider each one precious.
may we, too, consider each person precious.

For the cruel and hard-hearted; for all who abuse, destroy and undermine;

Silence

Lord, as you forgave those
who persecuted you, may we, too,
forgive our enemies, and pray for them.

For all who are the victims of war, terrorism, and political injustice;

Silence

Lord, may we recognise your face
in the face of everyone who is persecuted;
help us to realise
that when we respond with love
to the least of these,
we shall be responding to you.
Amen.

Hymn Christ be beside me

Finish with a shared Peace.

Susan Sayers
Reflective Services
40 quiet and gentle acts of worship

Refreshment

As you are gathering, sing 'Come, Holy Ghost' and 'Just as I am'. People can join in with the singing as soon as they are settled in stillness.

Recognise in this quietness, in God's attentive presence, the things you lack and need in your spiritual life. You can be quite honest with God about these – nothing is beyond his compassion or his forgiveness.

Silence

Lord, you alone can supply our deepest needs;
you alone can satisfy and fulfil.
Come, Holy Spirit of God,
come and fill us to overflowing.

Hymn Come, Holy Spirit, come

Remind yourself that to God we are very precious; well-known and well-loved. He knows our needs – even those which we may not be aware of. Imagine yourself as a pilgrim, footsore and weary. Jesus is looking after you with care and refreshment.

Silence

Listen now to the words of Psalm 23, which speak to us of the courteous and sensitive way that God refreshes us and caters for our needs.

Reading Psalm 23

This is the word of the Lord.
Thanks be to God.

Hymn O let the Son of God enfold you

Let the love of God enfold you. For this moment, nothing else is so important. If thoughts filter up to distract you, just acknowledge them and put them to one side. For the moment they don't have priority. Let God's enfolding love envelop your body, your mind and your spirit.

Silence

Anyone who trusts in the Lord
is like a tree planted by the waterside;
it thrusts out its roots into the stream
and is untroubled by heat or drought.
So the Lord says, 'Come to me, all you who are thirsty; come to me and I will refresh you.'

Lord, we pray for all in need of refreshment in their faith; for those whose prayer life is dry and parched;

Silence

Lord, may they drink
from your living water.

For those who are overwhelmed with doubts and misgivings about the faith in which they have been brought up;

Silence

Lord, as they drink from your living water,
may they find the reality of your presence
for themselves.

For those actively involved in ministry; that they may be given space and time to receive your necessary refreshment;

Silence

Lord, refresh them for their ministry
and for their own spiritual growth.

For all of us here today, and for those we spend time with each day;

Silence

Lord, you open your arms to welcome us.
and refresh us with many good things;
supplied with your gifts,
and empowered by your love,
may our lives tell others
the Good News that can give life;
life in abundance!
Amen.

Hymn Praise God from whom all blessings flow

Finish with a shared Peace.

Encouragement

While you are gathering, sing 'Laudate Dominum'. As you sing this song, feel solidarity with Christians in other continents.

Make yourself aware of the different parts your body, and relax them, one by one. Concentrate on the present moment; remember that it is held in being by God, and surrender to him your whole self.

Silence

Fear not, little flock, it is the Father's good pleasure to give you the kingdom.
Lord, we thank you that time and again
you encourage us on our journey.
Whenever weakness overtakes us,
whenever your will seems blocked,
whenever the next step looks treacherous,
whenever we reach the limits
of our resources;

then you encourage and strengthen our resolve,
you show us that with you
all things are possible,
you support us during the difficult moves,
and provide for our every need.

Oh Lord, our God,
without your encouragement
we would so often give up;
we thank you for empowering us
to work for the coming of your kingdom.

Hymn Lord of all hopefulness

Think over the times God has given you encouragement at low points of your life – through a friendship, or words spoken, or a particular event, or an experience of his presence in prayer. Thank God for such personal loving care.

Silence

Listen now to these words of encouragement from Luke's Gospel.

Reading Luke 12:22–32

This is the word of the Lord.
Thanks be to God.

Hymn Nada te turbe

Knowing that our heavenly Father loves and cares for all he has created, let us pray to him now for those who are feeling discouraged, and those who are experiencing failure.

Silence

Lord, give them your encouragement.

For those who are wary of stepping out in faith;

Silence

Lord, give them your encouragement.

For those whose self-esteem is low, and those who are despised;

Silence

Lord, give them your encouragement.

For those weakened by lives which are burdened with crisis after crisis;

Silence

Lord, give them your encouragement.

Lord, you have promised us
that you will be with us always,
to the end of the world.
With that promise to encourage us
in every situation,
may we walk your way with joy,
and infect the world with hope.
Amen.

Hymn You shall go out with joy

Finish with a shared Peace.

Humility

While gathering, start singing 'Be still, for the presence of the Lord'. When people arrive, let them settle in God's presence and then join in the singing.

Take time to tame your active mind to stillness. Keeping a relaxed but expectant stillness in your body is of value here; breathe naturally and regularly, and think of yourself breathing in God's peace with every breath.

Silence

Lord, we live in the middle of your remarkable creation;
all around us there is evidence
of your power, your glory,
your wisdom and your love.

And yet you came among us as one who serves;
instead of lording it over us,
you stand patiently at our door and knock.

Instead of imposing your presence on us,
you wait to be invited.
So now we invite you, Lord;
come to us; abide with us for ever.

In the opportunity of this unhurried quietness, invite God to live in you and through you, both now and for the future. Use your own, natural words, and remember that, although God is unnervingly powerful, he is also full of love and gentleness.

Silence

Hymn Alleluia, sing to Jesus

We do love you, Lord,
knowing that you first loved us.

In your humility you show us
the love that puts others before ourselves;
the love that has given self completely away;
the love that holds each one precious,
and treats each one with respect.

Listen now to these words from Mark's Gospel.

Reading Mark 10:35–45

Let us think over any areas where we may need to change our attitudes, in the light of this teaching. Let us ask the Lord to show us what these areas are, and empower us to realign our values where necessary.

Silence

Let us pray together now for all who are in positions of authority.

Silence

Lord, make us content to do only your will.

For those who have others dependent on them;

Silence

Lord, make us content to do only your will.

For those who live in terror because of political or personal victimisation;

Silence

Lord, in our weakness,
give us your strength.

For those whose countries are held in poverty through others' self-indulgence;

Silence

Lord, knowing our reliance on you
for everything,
and following your example
of loving service,
may we receive your strength and will
to practise the simplicity of humility,
in everything we do and say,
everywhere we go.
Amen.

Hymn Amazing grace

Finish with a shared Peace.

Power

As you are gathering, sing 'Be still, for the presence of the Lord' until everyone is attentive to the God of power and holiness.

Recognise that you are in the presence of the One who created the entire universe; the One who sees and understands all things.

Silence

Hymn Adoramus te, Domine

In this time of silent adoration, worship the Lord your God with all your mind and with all your heart and with all your strength. Don't allow anything to distract you from this essential duty and joy.

Silence

Maker of all;
sustainer of all;
we worship you,
we adore you,
for you are our God.

When I look at the sky, which you have made, at the moon and the stars, which you set in their places –
what are people, that you think of them;
mere people, that you care for them?

Think over the different aspects of our universe that remind you of God's power – perhaps as a waterfall; a thunderstorm; a volcano; the beginning of a new star. Think, too, of the power over sin and disease that Jesus showed.

Silence

O Lord, our Lord,
your greatness is seen in all the world!

Hymn This world you have made

Listen now to these readings, which tell of people's reaction to being shown God in the power of his glory.

Readings Ezekiel 3:22–24 (Ezekiel, the prophet); Luke 2:8–10 (The shepherds); Matthew 17:1–7 (Peter, James and John at the Transfiguration; Acts 2:6–11 (Paul at his conversion)

This is the word of the Lord.
Thanks be to God.

God still acts with great power in people's lives. Some find the thought of this terrifying. Do you hold back from him through fear? Remember that the God of power is also the God of love. 'Do not be afraid.'

Silence

Hymn Do not be afraid

Let us pray together now, in the presence of the almighty God who loves us, for a deeper understanding of the Lord of time and space.

Silence

Lord, have mercy on us.

For light to see more clearly our need of God;

Silence

Lord, have mercy on us.

For the courage to allow God access to every corner of our lives;

Silence

Lord, have mercy on us.

For the humility to give God the glory for all that he does through us;

Silence

Lord, have mercy on us.

Lord, we thank you
for the privilege of spending
this time in your presence.

We offer you now
the strength, the time and the resources
that you have given us.
Take us, Lord,
and use us for your glory.
Amen.

Hymn Take my life, and let it be

Finish with a shared Peace.

Susan Sayers
Reflective Services
40 quiet and gentle acts of worship

Acceptance

While you are gathering, sing 'Laudate Dominum' until everyone is settled in the presence of God. As people arrive, they can join in with the singing as soon as they are ready to.

Think of the different roles we play in our lives – you may be a child to one person, a parent to another, and employer to one, a friend to another. Accept all these aspects of yourself, and come before God, who sees all, hiding nothing and inventing nothing about yourself.

Silence

Lord we praise you
that in order to save us
you accepted the limitations of humanity;
in order to set us free
you accepted death by crucifixion;
in order to redeem us
you accepted the need
to pay the price for sin
in full,
and without condition.

Oh Lord, our God,
we thank you, and adore you.

Hymn A man there lived in Galilee

In thankfulness, think over the accepting love shown in Jesus, which carried on forgiving right through torture and execution; and continues forgiving us now, right through the times we reject his commands, ignore his will, or forget to honour him.

Silence

Lord, not only did you accept death in obedience to the Way of love;
but you also accept us,
just as we are,

and in full knowledge
of what we could be.

Listen now to these words of God, spoken both to the chosen people of Israel and also to us, the new Israel.

Reading Isaiah 43:1–7

This is the word of the Lord.
Thanks be to God.

Hymn Peace, perfect peace, is the gift

In stillness, let us allow God to nourish us, so that in accepting him as Lord of our lives we can love as he loves.

Silence

Lord, let your will be done in us and in your world. Show us where we have not yet fully accepted your ways.

Silence

Lord, let your will be done in us.

Bless the work of all peacemakers, and all involved in practical loving care.

Silence

Lord, let your will be done in us.

Encourage us when we discover that acceptance of your Way leads us to the cross.

Silence

Lord, let your will be done in us.

Lord, when we fail you, do not give up on us; when we turn away, turn us back to you.

Silence

Lord, let your will be done in us.

Hymn A new commandment

Finish with a shared Peace.

Creation

As you are gathering, sing 'Jubilate, everybody'. When enough people are present, you can sing it as a round if you like.

Lord of creation,
we rejoice in all that you have made;
heaven and earth are full of your glory!

Run your mind over some of the most beautiful places you have visited, or seen in pictures or on film. Think of them as the works of an artist, and let your pleasure in God's world lead you on to worship the artist himself.

Silence

Hymn This world you have made

Out of the darkness and void,
God is creating.
Out of chaos,
God is bringing order.
Out of the fragments we offer
God is creating wholeness.
Into despair,
God breathes hope;
into anxiety
God breathes peace;
into deadness
God breathes life.

With your body still and relaxed, but attentive, notice the stillness of things around you and feel part of the present moment, which is held in place by God's love.

Silence

Hymn Let all that is within me

Listen now to these words from John's Gospel.

Reading John 1:1–14

This is the word of the Lord.
Thanks be to God.

Think over the words you have been listening to: 'In the beginning was the Word: the Word was with God and the Word was God.' Jesus, then, is the Word of God; the Expression of God.

Silence

Heavenly Father, in Jesus we have seen your glory with a human face. Through Jesus, we pray for the world you have created in all its beauty and variety.

Silence

Lord, make us good stewards of all your gifts.

For the regions of rich growth and for the parched deserts, with all the life they need to support;

Silence

Lord, make us good stewards of all your gifts.

For the life you have given us, with our particular responsibilities and opportunities;

Silence

Lord, make us good stewards of all your gifts.

For our families, friends and neighbours, and all who provide for our needs;

Silence

Lord, make us good stewards of all your gifts.

Lord of creation,
we offer you our lives;
we ask that we may be
instruments of praise
in the words we speak,
in the things we do,
in the way that we live.
Amen.

Hymn Praise the Lord, ye heavens adore him

Finish with a shared Peace.

Eternity

While you are gathering, sing 'Spirit of mercy, truth and love', until everyone is settled and joining in the praise of God's everlasting loving kindness.

Try to put aside all thoughts of the past and the future. Be attentive to the present moment, where you are in stillness, in the company of your Lord and Saviour.

Silence

Before and after time,
there is God.
Where past and future are gathered,
there is God.
Beyond the death of the body,
there is God.

For you, O Lord, are everlasting,
faithful for ever and eternally present;
you are the great 'I AM' and we worship you.

Hymn Majesty

When we worship God we are living not only in time but in eternity as well. In this time of quietness, recognise this amazing truth, and know yourself to be in both dimensions, entirely through the grace and love of the everlasting God.

Silence

Along with all who worship God, both in this world and in heaven,
we give you the glory and praise
which you alone deserve.

Though we are all of us separate
in this moment of time,
in colour, in shape, and in place;
yet, through the power of the God we worship,
we are united in one body, and one spirit.
bound together in time and eternity.

Take time to feel solidarity with other Christians in different countries and in different cultures, all over the world. They are all our brothers and sisters. You are their brother or sister. Remember this as we pray in the silence: 'Our Father in heaven, may your name be hallowed.'

Silence

Listen now to John's Gospel.

Reading John 8:54–58

This is the word of the Lord.
Thanks be to God.

My brothers and sisters in Christ, let us pray now to the God who lives for ever. We remember with gratitude those we have loved and who have now passed through death into eternity.

Silence

You are the resurrection, and you are life.

We remember those who are approaching death, and commit them to your everlasting love and mercy.

Silence

You are the resurrection, and you are life.

We remember those who are fearful of dying, and those who are fearful of staying alive.

Silence

You are the resurrection, and you are life.

We remember the whole company of believers who have ever, and will ever, live;
with them we praise and glorify the Lord
who is alive, and reigns for ever
as our eternal King.
Blessed be God for ever!

Hymn Ubi caritas

Finish with a shared Peace.

Growth

As you are gathering, sing 'Open our eyes, Lord'. When people arrive, they should settle themselves to stillness and join in with the ongoing worship.

Think of yourself strongly rooted, like a tree with your roots sunk into the deep spring of God, which will never run dry. Draw inner life and peace from that spring now.

Silence

Blessed is anyone who trusts in the Lord:
such a person is like a tree by the waterside,
that thrusts its roots to the stream:
when the heat comes it has nothing to fear,
its foliage stays green;
untroubled in a year of drought,
it never stops bearing fruit.
Lord, deepen our trust,
that in you we may grow strong
and bear much fruit.

Hymn Make me a channel of your peace

Ask God to show you any branches of behaviour that need pruning; and any roots that you rely on, which lead only to puddles that will run dry. Allow God to nurture strong growth in you.

Silence

Listen now to these words of Jesus.

Reading John 15:1–8

This is the word of the Lord.
Thanks be to God.

Lord, in all your creation
we see the profusion of growth;
the variety of fruits:
the cycle of regeneration.

In every acorn
there is the potential for a forest;

in every apple pip
there is the potential for an orchard;
in every soul
there is the potential for your kingdom,
to be established,
full of peace, and joy, and love.
O Lord, may your kingdom come,
in us and in all creation.

In the attentive stillness, long for the kingdom of God to come in you and in the whole world.

Silence

Let us pray together for the growth of the kingdom; for many hearts to be alerted to their need of God, and fullness of life that he alone can give.

Silence

Lord, may your kingdom come.

For all who have put their trust in money, possessions and success, and feel the nudge of disillusion;

Silence

Lord, may your kingdom come.

For those in whom spiritual growth is fragile and vulnerable;

Silence

Lord, may your kingdom come.

The growing may be painful;
root-growth may be unseen;
we may sometimes prefer the seed we are
to the tree we might become.

Lord, give us courage for the growing,
that we may grow tall in your love
and bear fruit in abundance for your glory,
and for the good of your world.
Amen.

Hymn Will you come and follow me

Finish with a shared Peace.

Order

As everyone is gathering, sing 'Majesty' and 'God be in my head'. When you arrive, settle to stillness in the presence of God, and join in the ongoing worship.

As you breath in, think of yourself drawing in God's gift of life; as you breathe out, think of yourself exhaling all concern with Self. Breathe naturally and regularly.

Silence

Lord, we owe our entire existence to your constant love for us.
In you alone we live and move
and have our being.
Our genetic inheritance,
our genetic functioning:
all is designed and sustained
by the mastery of your hands
and the power of your love.

Not only in our own bodies, but throughout the whole of creation,
there is order and pattern,
structure and design,
balance and beauty.
O Lord our God, how excellent are your ways:
let everything that has breath
praise the Lord!

Hymn All creatures of our God and King

Let your whole being – body, mind and spirit – give thanks and praise to the God who designed you, made you and sustains your life, along with all living creatures throughout the world.

Silence

Listen now to these words from Psalm 104, rejoicing in the mastery and caring nature of God.

Reading Psalm 104:24–33

This is the word of the Lord.
Thanks be to God.

Let us praise together the God who brings order out of chaos. We praise him for all the times that good has emerged from evil in our lives, and difficulties have been overcome.

Silence

Lord, we thank you, and praise you.

We praise him for every argument that has been resolved; and every relationship which has been healed.

Silence

Lord, we thank you and we praise you.

We praise him for each time that confusion has given way to understanding: and fear to reassurance.

Silence

Lord, we thank you and we praise you.

We praise you, Lord,
for every time
the weak are treated with gentleness,
the lonely with affection,
the distressed with sympathy,
and the downtrodden with respect.

Your ways, Lord, are perfect;
may our lives,
ordered according to your will,
proclaim the beauty of your peace.
Amen.

Hymn God is working his purpose out

Finish with a shared Peace.

Protection

While everyone is gathering, have 'The Lord is my light' already being sung, so that as you arrive you settle yourself into stillness in the presence of God and join in the ongoing worship.

Here in the company of our Lord, we can let all our tension go, because we are completely safe. Slowly and deliberately, let yourself relax in the everlasting arms of the One who loves you, now and for ever.

Silence

In many ways the psalmists express their wonder at God's protection:
Lord, open our hearts to understand
the wonder of your love for us.

The Lord covers us with his feathers:
we find shelter under his wings.
The Lord is a strong rock;
he provides firm footing
so that our feet do not slip.
The Lord pulls us out of deep water;
in the mire of our distress he rescues us.
We need only to say, 'I am slipping',
and the Lord is there to hold us up.
Lord, however can we thank you
for your constant loving-kindness
and faithful care of us?

Hymn The King is among us

Know that in our heavenly Father's eyes we are his special children – accepted and loved. No matter how old we are, or how often we have failed or been rejected by others, our heavenly Father knows us personally by name, and he loves us.

Silence

Listen now to these words from Matthew's Gospel, where, through Jesus, we are shown God's loving protection.

Reading Matthew 14:22–33

This is the word of the Lord.
Thanks be to God.

Imagine yourself during the violent storm, in that boat with the disciples. Imagine yourself walking over the pounding waves to Jesus. What goes through your mind as you feel yourself sinking? How do you feel as Jesus catches hold of you and brings you to safety? Notice how calm the sea has become. How do you feel about Jesus now?

Silence

Knowing that our heavenly Father holds each person in his love, let us pray for those in various parts of the world who are in danger at the moment from war and terrorism.

Silence

Lord, protect them;
keep them eternally safe.

For the young and vulnerable who are sleeping rough in cities throughout the world;

Silence

Lord, protect them;
keep them eternally safe.

For all children whose mental, physical or emotional health is endangered by abuse or neglect;

Silence

Lord, protect them;
keep them eternally safe.

O Lord our God, we rejoice that whatever happens to us
nothing at all can ever separate us
from the love of God
which is in Christ Jesus our Lord.
Alleluia!

Hymn Jesus, name above all names

Finish with a shared Peace.

Faithfulness

While everyone is gathering, sing 'I will enter his gates'. As people arrive, they should settle their minds and bodies, and join in with the worship when they are ready.

God has promised us that where two or three are gathered together in his name, he will be there among them.
Holy God,
help me draw near to worship you
with all my heart,
and with all my mind.
and with all my strength.

Let us offer the Lord our full attentiveness. Let your body be relaxed, and breathe naturally and regularly. Every thought that filters up can be turned into worship by offering it to God. Let the Lord himself teach us and empower us to worship in the best way.

Silence

Hymn Give thanks with a grateful heart

Lord, we give you thanks and we praise you,
for in spite of our weakness
and in spite of our poverty,
you are always faithful in your love for us.

Though we let you down, and turn away from your presence,
yet you never ever forget us,
never give up on us, never stop loving us.

Hear in your mind this great promise that the Lord makes to us: 'Look, I am with you always'. Let the words take root in you, not just for now, but for the situations and relationships in your life where Jesus' presence would make all the difference.

Silence

Listen now to these words of the psalmist, praising God for his faithfulness and abiding love.

Reading Psalm 103

This is the word of the Lord.
Thanks be to God.

As children of our loving heavenly Father, let us pray together for those who feel let down or slighted by someone they love; for all whose faithfulness is being severely tested.

Silence

Lord, increase our faith.
and keep us faithful.

For those who find it hard to believe in a completely faithful God; all who are afraid to trust in case they are let down;

Silence

Lord, increase our faith.
and keep us faithful.

For those who have wandered so far from your way, that they feel themselves beyond your forgiveness and love;

Silence

Lord, increase our faith,
and keep us faithful.

In stillness, let us dedicate ourselves again to following the Lord faithfully each day of our lives. You may find it helpful to use these words of St Patrick: 'Lord, may I know you more clearly, love you more dearly and follow you more nearly day by day.' Or use your own words – it is not the words, but the longing and the love that are important.

Silence

Hymn Bind us together, Lord

Finish with a shared Peace.

Devotion

As people are gathering, sing 'Jesus, thou joy of loving hearts'.

God is already here among us.
He was here waiting for us to arrive
and he set out with us as we left;
let us quieten and still ourselves
to recognise his presence.

Make your body completely still, without tension. Notice the stillness of things around you. Think of them being poised in a moment of eternity. Remember that all this existence is within the mind of God. Sense his cradling of this moment in his hand.

Silence

Though the mountains may fall and the hills turn to dust,
the love of our God shall stand.
Though even a mother should forsake her baby,
I will never forsake you, my child.
Though heaven and earth pass away,
my words shall never pass away.

Listen to the word of God, spoken through the prophet, Isaiah.

Reading Isaiah 51:12–16

This is the word of the Lord.
Thanks be to God.

Think of the night sky and the distances shown by stars. Think of God stretching out our universe and laying the foundations of our planet Earth. Think of him knowing, from the beginning, all history and all lives. Your life. This moment.

Silence

Great and faithful God, it is your nature to accompany us;
to grieve at the wounding,
to share in the joy,
to gather us up when we stumble,
to calm us when we are afraid,
to nudge us into action,
to curb our excesses.
Through days and lifetimes
you are Emmanuel – God with us.

Call to mind any situations during the coming week which are likely to be difficult and demanding. Invite God into the area and commend all those involved to his guidance and protection. Call to mind anything in your behaviour which concerns you. Invite God into this province and allow him to work there. Be prepared to listen to the ideas that come into your mind while you are praying. Measure them against God's goodness and love.

Silence

Hymn We will lay our burden down

Wherever you call us, Lord, our God,
we want to be ready and willing to go.
Whenever you need us, Lord, our God,
we want to be available and attentive.
Whoever turns out to be our neighbour in need,
we want to be happy to serve, without exceptions.

Live within us, Lord our God,
so that we notice with your discernment,
respond with your compassion,
and speak with your integrity.
In our lives and in our world,
let your kingdom come.
Amen.

Finish with a shared Peace.

Patience

As you are gathering, sing 'Holy, holy, holy is the Lord'. As people arrive, they should settle themselves to stillness and join in the worship.

Think over with sadness the many ways we are unworthy of the patient love of God. Lay these times before him and ask his forgiveness.

Silence

Hymn O Lord, your tenderness

Take time to accept the Lord's forgiveness and be assured of his continuing love for you. Allow God to make you into the kind of person he hopes you will become.

Silence

Lord, you are so patient with us;
so often we lag behind your will,
or race ahead with our own plans;
so often we do the right things
for the wrong reasons,
and fail to obey your will.
Yet time and again you search us out
and find us,
time and again you forgive us
and bring us safely home.

Most patient Saviour,
we love you and adore you.

Hymn I love you, Lord

Listen now to these words of Peter in his second letter, and James in his letter.

Readings 2 Peter 3:8, 9; James 5:7–1 1

This is the word of the Lord.
Thanks be to God.

We tend not to think too much about the time when Jesus will come again in glory. Spend time now reflecting on the knowledge that it will certainly happen, yet all we know about the date is that we will not be expecting it. How ready are you for this? Are you prepared for it every day?

Silence

Let us pray together for the coming of the kingdom, that we may live each day as if it were our last.

Silence

Lord, be patient with us
and teach us your ways.

We pray for a more accepting love, so that we may be more patient with those who annoy and irritate us.

Silence

Lord, be patient with us
and teach us your ways.

We pray for those whom we irritate and annoy, and ask for sensitivity in recognising our own faults and weaknesses.

Silence

Lord, be patient with us
and teach us your ways.

We pray for your blessing and anointing on all who need patience in their work.

Silence

Lord, be patient with us
and teach us your ways.

Lord, through our sufferings
teach us to persevere
and put our trust in you;
through any unjust criticisms for doing your will,
teach us patient and joyful acceptance.
As we run the race that is set before us,
let us run with patience,
delighting only in doing your will.

Hymn Do not be afraid

Finish with a shared Peace.

Thanksgiving

Great Spirit of God,
abundant and unique,
boundless and intimate,
you are our God,
and we are your children.
You are our shepherd,
and we are the sheep of your pasture.

Hymn Be still, for the presence of the Lord

Use this space to adore and worship the God who made you and sustains your life. Remember his goodness to you over the years. Remember his mercy. Don't ask anything. Give thanks instead. Tell him your love.

Silence

Glory be to the one true God.
Glory to the Father.
Glory to Jesus, the Christ.
Glory to the Holy Spirit.
As God was in the beginning;
as God is, now;
as God will be for ever.
Amen.

Reading Revelation 5:11–14

This is the word of the Lord.
Thanks be to God.

For frost and cobwebs, snowflakes and blossom,
for all that is fragile, delicate and of fleeting beauty,
we praise our loving God.

Silence

For gravity, magnetism, refraction and all the natural, physical laws which order our universe,
we praise our loving God.

Silence

For microorganisms and cell structure, for all that is microscopic and intricately balanced,
we praise our loving God.

Silence

For the supportive network of human relationships, for all that befriends, encourages, challenges and refreshes us,
we praise our loving God.

Silence

For unexpected kindness and unexpected loveliness, for all that surprises us with joy and lifts our spirits,
we praise our loving God.

Silence

Hymn Praise, my soul, the King of heaven

Think of yourself being bathed in God's sunlight of goodness and love. As the light surrounds you, know that you are cocooned in the tender affection of the One who loved you into being, delights in you, understands you and feels with you.

Silence

Almighty, all-seeing, all-merciful God,
make me more responsive to you,
develop my sensitivity to your presence,
deepen my awareness of your love,
that I may give you honour, glory and praise
with all of my heart,
with all of my mind,
and with all of my strength
for ever.
Amen.

Finish with a shared Peace.

Rededication

As people are gathering, sing 'Seek ye first'.

O God, both here and everywhere,
in time and eternity,
both around and within,
we worship you.

O God, both near and transcendant,
active and unchanging,
giving and forgiving,
we worship you.

As you wait on God in stillness, know that you are in the presence of the God who appeared to Moses and led the ancient people of Israel to freedom. You are in the presence of Jesus, who walked the roads of Palestine and Samaria. God was 'I AM' throughout history, and he is 'I AM' now. As you breathe in and out, drawing life from the air, think of yourself breathing God's breath of life, his Spirit, deep into your being.

Silence

Listen to these words of advice, spoken by Jesus.

Reading Luke 12:27–31

This is the word of the Lord.
Thanks be to God.

When our lives become overcrowded with importance, and the diary is full, and the weeks are too short;
then get in our way and disturb our routine
until we remember that you, Lord God,
are the centre and the foundation.

When the troubles and changes dismember our peace, and the future intimidates us,
and the past haunts us;

then whisper your truth in the core of our being
until we remember that you, Lord God, are almighty and here.

When we become complacent and think we are in control,
and strangers don't fit,
and all change is threat;
then break us apart;
scatter our assumptions in the gale of your breath;
teach us to live in the unpredictable freedom of your Spirit.

Hymn When I feel the touch

Let us call to mind the different areas of our lives and the different roles we play. Invite God to reign in every situation and in every relationship. Are there any areas or activities which jar as you look at them in God's light? Are there any opportunities you are avoiding or discounting?

Silence

Father God, all that we are lies open before you,
our achievements and disappointments,
our dreams and misgivings,
our commitments and responsibilities,
our gifts and weaknesses.

Take us as we are,
where we are,
who we are,
and make us fully ourselves,
strong in your strength and rich with your love,
as we serve you alone,
the God of our making,
with heart and mind and spirit
in all that we think and say and do.
Amen.

Finish with a shared Peace.

Before a meeting

As people are gathering, sing 'Breath on me, Breath of God'.

Lord God, we have come to gather in your presence.
Deliberately we do this first
before the business of our meeting
and before we discuss anything at all.

Before we speak
we have come to listen.
Before we make decisions
we have come to discern your will.

Quieten our hearts to hear you, holy God.

Recollect that our God already knows and loves each person here, and each of those we all represent. He is already familiar with the agenda and the concerns before us. Let us recognise our dependence on God for life itself, and give him full authority over our thoughts, words and actions.

Silence

God of wisdom, God of power, you alone have the words of eternal life.
We thirst for your goodness,
and come to you for drink.
We hunger for your righteousness,
and come to you for food.

Hymn As pants the hart for cooling streams

Hear these words of the psalmist which remind us of our priorities.

Reading Psalm 127:1

This is the word of the Lord.
Thanks be to God.

Make a conscious effort to set aside all prejudice and any preconceived ideas. Recognise that we all act and react to some extent out of our past experience and our past wounding. Invite the God of power and tenderness to transform any negative experiences you may have had, so that they can be used positively.

Silence

As we prepare for the work before us let us pray to the one, true, living God. From a critical and destructive attitude to others,
Lord, set us free.

From empire-building and selfishness,
Lord, set us free.

From too much talking and too little attentive listening,
Lord, set us free.

From a quarrelsome spirit,
Lord, set us free.

In ways of integrity and honesty,
Lord, lead us.

In ways of compassion and understanding,
Lord, lead us.

In ways of discernment and expectancy,
Lord, lead us.

So that in all we discuss and decide,
your kingdom may come,
and your will be done,
on earth as it is in heaven.

For the kingdom,
and the power,
and the glory,
are yours for ever and ever.
Amen.

Finish with a shared Peace.

Endings

Lord God, our maker,
all-powerful and all-seeing:
we worship you.

Lord God, our redeemer,
all-loving and compassionate:
we worship you.

Lord God, our comforter,
enabling and transforming:
we worship you.

Before the beginning,
and after the end,
and for ever,
you are the one, true God,
and we worship and adore you.

Hymn Father, we adore you

Together we have worked and relaxed in the presence of God. Together we have travelled on our journey of faith. Now, before we take leave of one another and go our different ways, let us be still in God's company, and reflect on our time together.

Think over what you have heard, seen, thought, said and done which has challenged or helped you. Bring to mind the insights you have gained, and the friendships. Bring to mind the opportunities presented to act lovingly, patiently and with forgiveness. Recognise any regrets, offer them and learn from them.

Silence

For the companionship we have enjoyed,
we give thanks.
For the ideas we have shared and explored,
we give thanks.
For the challenges that have unsettled our assumptions,
we give thanks.

For the opportunities to practise patience and forbearance,
we give thanks.
For all we have learnt and understood,
we give thanks.
For all that has been achieved,
we give thanks.
For the needs that have been met,
we give thanks.

For any unkindness
we ask your forgiveness.
For any hurt
we ask your restoring.
For any confusion
we ask your direction.
For, Lord God, in you alone
we place our trust.

Reading Romans 12:9–21

This experience we have shared is part of us now and will in some way affect the way we live. As we disperse let us recollect, in God's company, the situations and relationships to which we are returning. Remember that God's guidance and love are unlimited by place or time or circumstances. Reflect on the needs and joys, responsibilities and privileges you will be facing, and welcome into it all the God who knows and loves us.

Silence

Hymn O Lord, hear my prayer

Make us free to love you with heart and mind and strength.
Make us free to love our neighbour as we love ourselves.
In all we think and speak and do
may your kingdom come and your will be done. Amen.

Finish with a shared Peace.